PARTNERSHIP WITH PARE
Supporting NASEN _ _ _

Articles by Parents and Professionals

edited by

Sheila Wolfendale

Chair of
NASEN's Partnership with Parents Interest Group

A NASEN Publication

Published in 1997
© NASEN's Partnership with Parents Interest Group

ISBN 0 906730 92 9

Published by NASEN Enterprises Ltd.
NASEN Enterprises is a company limited by guarantee, registered in England and Wales. Company No. 2637438.

Further copies of this book and details of NASEN's many other publications may be obtained from the Publications Department at its registered office:
NASEN House, 4/5 Amber Business Village, Amber Close, Amington, Tamworth, Staffs., B77 4RP
Tel: 01827 311500; Fax: 01827 313005;
email: welcome@nasen.org.uk

Copy edited by Mike Hinson.
Cover design by Graphic Images.
Typeset in Times New Roman by NASEN Enterprises Ltd.

PARTNERSHIP WITH PARENTS IN ACTION
Supporting NASEN Policy

CONTENTS

Membership of the Parental Partnership Interest Group Committee 1996-1997:

Sheila Wolfendale (Chair); Katy Simmons (Hon Secretary); Sally Beveridge (Hon Treasurer); Karen Cockerill; Lindsay Haines; Jeff Hughes; Helen Jones; Joyce Kynaston; Jane Little; Stephanie Lorenz; Carolyn Morley.

Acknowledgements

The editor and publishers gratefully acknowledge the help and advice of:
- John Wright, Director of IPSEA [Independent Panel of Special Education Advice, 4 Ancient House Mews, Woodbridge, Suffolk, IP12 1DH] in preparing an explanation of recent legislative changes;
- Mike Hinson, Chair of NASEN's Publications Sub-Committee, 1992-1997.

1 - Preface

This short publication celebrates the advent of NASEN's **Partnership with Parents** policy and aims to support its implementation by bringing together in print, the experiences and views of parents and professionals who spoke at two NASEN foundation conferences, one at Haydock Park in November 1995 and the second, held in March 1996 in Crawley, West Sussex. The second conference was organised in partnership with the West Sussex Parent Partnership Scheme.

We hope that readers will find the personal accounts of parents and other workers inspiring and illuminating. They graphically describe the challenges upon parents of children with special needs and the attempts by professionals, paid workers, to work in partnership with parents. The context to this work is now the *1994 Code of Practice* which sets out principles of partnership. The Department for Education and Employment has funded, through GEST (Grants for Education Support and Training) a three year (1994 - 1997) project to establish parent partnership schemes in most LEAs, and the accounts from Cheshire and West Sussex describe the operation of their schemes. From both these county areas parent partnership officers, parents, SENCOs (Special Educational Needs Co-ordinators in Schools) came together to provide a lively account of the setting up and operation of their schemes. Doris Thompson compellingly tells of her parental experiences.

As described in NASEN's magazine *Special!* (Summer 1996), the two conferences attracted 'full houses' of parents, teachers, Portage workers, parent partnership officers, educational psychologists, LEA officers, voluntary organisation workers. Conference evaluations were highly positive about the strength of the speakers' commitment to working in partnership. Speakers and participants also found the days useful to network with each other and came away with a number of messages about practical ways to implement co-operative ways of working with and on behalf of children.

In this report, we also include the written accounts of the other speakers at both conferences: Sheila Wolfendale examines the 'vision and the reality of partnership'; Katy Simmons looks at the new SEN

Tribunal system, and Jeff Hughes gives the results of the NASEN survey into views on partnership of parent and professional members of NASEN. Jeff's findings affirm the need for a policy, now adopted by NASEN, which can help to realise partnership in practice.

A list of references and further reading is provided and, in the Appendices, readers will find a Glossary of Terms (a brief explanation of jargon and technical terms!); a summary table explaining the section changes of the *1996 Education Act*, which has now incorporated the *1993 Education Act* as well as other education acts of the last few years; a list of addresses and further contacts, and, in Appendix 3, we have reproduced in full NASEN's policy for **Partnership with Parents**.

Supporting NASEN to implement the policy on 'Partnership with Parents'

The policy, reproduced in Appendix 3 was also printed in the Summer 1996 issue of *Special!*. It is further echoed in these two extracts from NASEN's 1996 Mission Statement:

'...to encourage the development of policy at local, national and international level'
and
'maximum participation by parents and carers must be secured in order to achieve partnership in education'.

Naturally NASEN wants to see the **Parents in Partnership** policy enacted and implemented at these levels and for NASEN members, whether parents, professionals or both, to reach out to foster partnership practice in SEN assessment and in decision making over provision. Sharing existing good practice is paramount to celebrate success and to inspire the spread of such practice.

The NASEN **Parent Partnership Interest Group** was formed at the Haydock Park conference. The Interest Group is charged with the responsibility of assisting NASEN to implement its **Partnership with Parents** policy in a variety of ways. This publication is an initiative of the Interest Group and all the Committee members (see page 4) have assisted in some way towards its publication. Especial thanks go to

Karen Cockerill for typing the whole manuscript. The editor takes final responsibility for the booklet. The Committee, comprising parents and professionals met on four occasions between January 1996 and January 1997, and the Interest Group is steadily building a membership.

We are keen to attract and recruit members who can help foster partnership with parents in their own local and work settings, and we welcome interest, active involvement and good ideas from NASEN members to join and help the Interest Group. Please contact Katy Simmons, PO Box 1933, Marlow, Bucks., SL7 3TS for further details.

2 - 'Partnership with Parents - a NASEN Survey'
Jeff Hughes

In the early 1990s when NASEN (the National Association for Special Educational Needs) was formed from NCSE (the National Council for Special Education) and NARE (the National Association for Remedial Education) a concessionary, but limited, subscription was offered to parents of children and young people with special educational needs.

When NASEN's Membership Committee examined its concessionary membership list in 1992 it found only 16 'parent' members. Although a few branches had parents on their Committees and held meetings relevant to parents, the majority of others had not considered parents as members. It seemed that, although NASEN said that it wanted parents as members, it knew little about its parent members and very little was being done to attract them.

After protracted discussions during 1993 and early 1994, NASEN's General Assembly (which is comprised of representatives of all branches) decided that it wished the Association to be seen as more welcoming to parent members and to actively promote partnership with them. The concessionary subscriptions would now offer the same benefits as for all other members, and a survey would be undertaken to ask what parents might want of professionals and NASEN. A Working Party was set up, chaired by Sheila Wolfendale, with Mike Hinson (at the time NASEN's temporary Executive Secretary) as secretary and as liaison with the General Assembly and Executive Committee. Its brief was to produce a policy statement on 'working with parents' to put before the General Assembly. The final policy document was ratified by the Assembly on 25th March 1995.

A first draft of the Survey, which included only questions asking parents about their needs was modified by the Membership Committee to include questions about what professionals might need to help them work with parents. The second draft, which was circulated to the Assembly and the Parent Partnership Working Party, prompted considerable discussion about its wording, especially possible misinterpretations of 'professional', 'parent' and 'child' and the likely over-complication of the survey form if we tried to avoid them.

Some minor changes were made and, late in 1994, a four-sided leaflet was given to every NASEN branch for circulation especially to parents. Respondents were asked to indicate whether they were a 'parent', answering all ten questions, or a 'professional', answering only six questions. Delegates at the Parental Partnership Interest Group's two 'Working Together' conferences in 1995 were also asked to participate. A final total of 219 forms were returned, of which 88 were from parents of children and young people with special educational needs, including 31 respondents who were both parents and professionals.

Parents' needs
The first section of the questionnaire focussed on parents' views. The question **'What concerns you most about your child's special educational needs?'** revealed most concern about the appropriateness or quality of provision (28 responses). Lack of resources (15), fear of segregation (12), and lack of information (10) were followed by concern that mainstream teachers did not understand special educational needs (9). Although both groups of parents expressed greatest concern about provision (20 parents, 8 parents who were professionals), parents who were also professionals were next most concerned about integration (6) and resources (6) while the non-professional group saw resources (9) as second.

When asked **'What information do you feel you most need?'** clear, open, realistic information was top of the parents' list (12). While parents who were also professionals also placed curriculum organisation (5) top those who were not professionals wanted to know about the help available (7) and the support which would be appropriate (7). Information on independent assessment and tuition (2) and advocacy (2) was quite low in the parents' priorities. Asked **'What guidance or support do you feel you need most?'** help and support for parents (16) came top with meetings and support groups (11) and information on choices (9) next, mainly for non-professional parents.

The most frequent response to **'How has membership of NASEN helped you as the parent or carer of a child or young person with special educational needs?'** was, for both groups of parents, 'I'm not a member' (26). Second highest for parents who were not professionals was recognising there are limits to resources (10) with information (6) second highest for parents who were also professionals. Only a few respondents specifically mentioned NASEN's books (4) and meetings (3) as helpful while seven respondents thought NASEN too focussed towards professionals.

Professionals' needs

The second section, on professionals' needs, was almost exclusively completed by respondents who were professionals. The top response to **'What concerns professions most about working with the parents or carers of children and young people with special educational needs?'** was communicating effectively with parents (31) followed by lack of resources (24), lack of time with parents (23) and lack of knowledge (16). Dealing with parents who cannot support their children (14) or have unrealistic expectations (10) were also high priorities.

Knowledge of special educational needs (37) and being open to families' needs (36) were the most popular responses to **'What information do you feel that professionals need most when they work with the parents or carers of children and young people who have special educational needs?'** Communication and listening skills (19), knowledge of entitlements and rights (18) and access to other agencies (14) also gained substantial responses.

The clear concern of the professionals when asked **'What training do you feel that professionals need most before they work with the parents or carers of children and young people with special**

educational needs?' was for counselling and listening skills (72). Information on special educational needs (23) and training on how to meet special educational needs (23) were also substantial concerns. Being sensitive to parents' needs was first on the parents' list (7) but the fourth priority for professionals (13).

Training courses and lectures (55) were ahead of other forms of information updating (39) in response to **'What could NASEN offer which would be most useful to the professionals who work with the parents of children and young people who have special educational needs?'** Enabling professionals and parents to communicate better was third for professionals (15) but top of the list for parents who were also professionals (7).

Partnership

All three groups agreed that trust, honesty and openness (57) and good communication skills (47) were most important when asked **'Please tell us what is most important in making a partnership between parents and professionals work'**. Mutual respect (19), working together (18), clear, agreed aims (16) and listening to parents (15) came ahead of time (13).

'What can NASEN do to help?' produced fewer responses than most earlier questions with parent support groups (21), training courses (19), information leaflets (18) and other publications (15) at the top of the list. Bringing parents and professionals together was the first priority of parents (5) but only fourth for professionals (11).

Discussion

As one of a number of activities aimed at developing NASEN, the survey was intended as a step in the process rather than an academically-rigorous device. Discussions which took place at this time in the General Assembly, Membership Committee, and elsewhere were deciding how NASEN was to develop. That the General Assembly decided to focus efforts on recruitment of schools and parents indicated NASEN's pragmatic and philosophical priorities.

It was realised, at the time that the survey was conceived, that there would be limitations to the data obtained from a relatively limited sample. With circulation only through NASEN the respondents would most likely represent that minority of parents and professionals who are active, aware and articulate.

Having decided to keep the questionnaire form simple, differences between respondents in their interpretation of the questions were likely. Similarly, because there were only a few general questions, information which might have been collected by more detailed questioning would be missed.

The value of the survey as a means of raising awareness was felt to be almost as valuable as any data it produced. This was underlined when those sections which referred to NASEN suffered from the respondents' lack of knowledge about NASEN, its aims and activities. This was the more surprising when the questionnaire had been handed out either by active NASEN members or at NASEN conferences!

Some members of the NASEN Membership Committee expressed a hope that this questionnaire would be the first of a series which would sample the wishes of members and potential members. Regular, and more focussed, sampling of NASEN members might guide NASEN's policy, services and activities as part of a programme of 'satisfaction surveys'. Likewise, research into the views and needs of non-members could be linked to member recruitment campaigns, but getting in contact with a representative sample could prove difficult.

Although quality and resources were the greatest concerns of parents answering Question One, when responses to all the questions were examined, responses which mentioned resource issues were, overall, least frequent from both parents and professionals. The highest priorities of both groups appeared to be the availability of information and training.

Special educational needs is sometimes portrayed as an area of confrontation, yet the survey does not seem to offer much evidence to support such a view. The emphasis on information and training suggests that reaching for successful decisions is uppermost in everyone's mind. Indeed, the lack of interest in second opinions could be taken to indicate a reasonable level of confidence in both the assessment process and the work of professionals. We should, perhaps, remember that the vast majority of children have their special educational needs identified and met without dispute.

The implications for NASEN of this survey seem to fall into two parts. Firstly, it is clear that the message about NASEN's aims and activities is missing a significant portion of those it wishes to reach. Secondly, there is a need for simple and accessible information about special educational needs for both parents and professionals. How NASEN does this remains to be seen but it has the right vehicles in the form of *Special!*, the *British Journal of Special Education, Support for Learning*, the wide range of books it publishes, the courses and seminars it organises, and the meetings and other activities of its local branches.

The Cheshire Experience
3 - A Parent's Experience
Doris Thompson

I am a teacher by profession, but I'm here today as a mother of three boys who are all statemented as having special educational needs.

My oldest boy is Steven. He's 12 years old, is dyspraxic (has developmental dyspraxia) and is in mainstream education.

Stuart, my middle boy, is ten years old. He has a severe language-speech disorder and moderate/severe learning difficulties. He's in a special school for MLD (moderate learning difficulties) children.

Philip, my youngest, is like his oldest brother, dyspraxic. He's in Year 3 in a mainstream school, with support.

It was apparent from a very early age that Stuart had problems. The most obvious was the lack of language. He was statemented while at nursery school and was placed in a language unit attached to a mainstream school.

Steven's difficulties were becoming apparent too. An intelligent boy, but his work was not matching his ability. His handwriting in particular was very unco-ordinated. He was labelled lazy and untidy and was put under such pressure that he came to a complete standstill in his Year 1 class. He was seen by an educational psychologist who gave advice to boost his confidence and get him working once more, but he didn't know why he should be experiencing these problems. Steven's balance and general co-ordination were also not good, and so I did the rounds of the clinics to have his eyesight, hearing and balance checked but all were found to be within the norm for his age. (Steven could do the general balancing tests that clinics do - finger on nose, standing on toes, walking a straight line - without too much difficulty). So although I'd seen at least four different people, all very willing to help, none of them could say what the real problem was. Now to Philip, who was the catalyst to set a lot of things in motion. His language and walking were very delayed, and knowing of Stuart's language problems, I quickly got in touch with a speech therapist.

As soon as she saw him, she asked if he always walked like that (shades of Steven). A strange observation you might think for a speech therapist, but she was obviously aware that sometimes speech and co-ordination problems can go together (I didn't at that time). She urged me to see a physiotherapist who might be able to help.

She certainly did. She came out and not only assessed Philip as having developmental dyspraxia but listened to my concerns about Steven. She became very interested in what I was saying and agreed to see Steven too.

She thought Steven was a 'classic' 'clumsy child' (not a good term, but it is used).

From then on things began to move. The physiotherapist arranged for all the boys to see the paediatrician, who agreed with her assessment of Steven and Philip, and arranged for an occupational therapist to come out and see them both.

Steven had changed schools when he entered the juniors, and his new school had encountered the same problems his infant school had, but refused to put a label on him. They wanted to find out exactly what his problems were first, so they'd arranged for an educational psychologist to see him.

When the physiotherapist knew this she arranged to ring the educational psychologist and talk to him to explain just what dyspraxia meant and the difficulties that would entail for a child. This meant the educational psychologist, instead of working in the dark, knew what he was looking for and could suggest solutions that would help Steven's specific problems.

The occupational therapist and physiotherapist had joint sessions with Steven, and because of the communication between the therapists, educational psychologist and school, the maximum progress was made.

A great difference was seen in Steven within a short time and a resultant growth in self-confidence.

This improvement has continued into his secondary school, where school and the educational psychologist have continued to talk and work together with Steven and home. And what of Philip? The physiotherapist made a priority case for his early admission to nursery. There too the educational psychologist was able to work with the knowledge of what the problem was. He got Philip into a very special (in all senses) nursery on a part-time basis, where the occupational therapist, the physiotherapist and the speech therapist were part of the curriculum and incorporated into every learning situation. Regular sessions with parents and the educational psychologist meant that everyone could exchange ideas and the best placement for Philip found. It was decided he would be able to cope with mainstream schooling, with support. This he has done, not without some set-backs occasionally, but with slow and steady progress.

All this was possible because of the opportunities for **all** the experts (health and educational) and parents to talk **together**, not separately, to us.

Stuart transferred from the mainstream language unit to a special school with a language unit. We have taken him to an educational psychologist, he's had a C.A.T. scan, and he's been seen by different therapists. All have done their best, but no one has come up with an answer. He has a multitude of problems, which need to be tackled together. This can only be done if all the experts come together, to talk about their findings to each other. Then we might begin to find an answer. A written report, of perhaps a dozen lines or so, does not give a true picture of a child's difficulties. School is trying magnificently to meet his needs, but I always have the feeling that somewhere we've missed something vital, that if we did have a real meeting, not just of school, parents and educational psychologist, but of all the other agencies who have seen Stuart separately, we might finally begin to unlock Stuart's potential.

After all, that is what has happened with my other two boys. The change in their perception of themselves, their school work and their everyday lives generally has been little short of dramatic. All this has been due to the fact that **all** the agencies came together to try and find the answer. No one agency was left to stumble in the dark. They met together with us, the parents, and **all** of us put forward our findings and ideas, to maximise the help our children needed.

I know it is expensive and time-consuming to do this, but oh, the benefits! And in the long run, it is a lot less of a waste of time, money and a child's life and ability.

4 - The GEST Parent Partnership Scheme
Linda Caldecott (Parent Partnership Officer)

The majority of parents tell us that their experience of partnership could be improved if communication and information-sharing between partners were improved. Partners keep in touch in a variety of ways at different times: letters, reports, documents and by talking to each other. Communication is at its best when there is genuineness, respect and empathy. Parents tell us that they value 'openness' most.

A minority of parents feel that they would benefit from personal support. Many parents have not had contact with a support group nor have thought about the need for a Named Person. However, those parents who have experienced support value it and it is important to share this with parents, who have not considered support themselves.

Information

Parents report that they are not well informed about special educational needs, particularly at the earlier stages of concern (pre-school and school based stages). At Stages 4 and 5 of the *Code of Practice* (see page 47), they would also like more information from the LEA. Parents feel excluded when they do not understand what is happening; they may not understand and this may lead to conflict or lack of opportunity.

Access to information about special educational needs

Information needs to be shared early in order that parents are well informed before they become involved in special needs procedures. Simple descriptions can be given early on 'signposting' steps in the process and other sources of information, which are more detailed.

Perhaps all information does not need to be translated into community languages but the service of interpreters needs to be made available as is presently the case in Warrington. In other areas of Cheshire arrangements are made ad hoc. The Racial Equality Council is recommending that a countywide interpreter service should be established. This idea has support from other services, who work closely with parents.
- All parents in Cheshire receive a Personal Child Health Record (PCHR).
- All parents have contact with schools.
- Some parents use libraries, clinics etc.
- A few parents have contact with the LEA at the statutory stages.

We have developed two new main sources of information about special educational needs:
- A leaflet that will be included in the PCHR. This has been developed with South Cheshire Health Trust, which will adopt it and produce it as part of their system of informing parents. This leaflet needs to be offered to other Trusts, Health Authorities in Cheshire.
- A parents' file, guiding them through special needs procedures and giving information about support. This file, with a video that explains the school based stages, was given to schools at half-day conferences which began in Spring 1996. Schools were asked to consider their arrangements for parents of children with special educational needs and encouraged to make the video and file available to parents. Schools have been encouraged to add to the file and to 'own it'.

We have been sharing other examples of information for parents at Stages 4 and 5 with LEA officers, sharing with them the views of parents about information at these stages. Any changes that might be made would aim to make parents feel that they are part of the process at these stages e.g. helpful forms for them to keep their own records of their involvement with the LEA.

Plain English
One of the LEA statementing officers attended a day's training in

Coventry, with one of the parent partnership officers. We have recommended to the education officer responsible for special needs county wide that other staff in special services might find this training very helpful and that plain English training should be arranged for personnel who write to parents.

Communication

Parents would like to have more openness in their communication with the LEA. Many parents have told us that they would like to improve their relationship with the Named Officer. They understand that this is the officer who keeps in touch with them and would like more personal contact.

We have passed on ideas for the development of the role of Named Officer and there has been some training arranged by SENJIT (SEN Joint Training Initiative) in London which was attended by LEA officers.

Some parents are aware that they can ask to see policy documents of the LEA as well as of schools. Policies need to be written in such a way that parents can understand them. Some consultation in the development of policies could be considered. Strathclyde LEA routinely produce policies in partnership with parents.

Support

- Contact a Family, the national charity, has agreed that we can use the guidelines that they have developed to help parents set up their own support groups. This will be included in the school file and has also been circulated to individual parents in Cheshire. In the final year of funding, the parent partnership scheme might work more directly to help parents of children with MLD (moderate learning difficulties) and EBD (emotional and behavioural difficulties) to set up support groups.
- Parents will be able to find out about local and national support groups from the school file. The parent partnership scheme has obtained leaflets from local groups to circulate to schools.
- Support at the statutory stages is being developed as the Named Person Scheme.

Collaboration between the LEA and the parent partnership scheme is essential to make sure that the scheme survives beyond GEST funding.

Training

Parents access information about special educational needs from a variety of professionals at pre-school and they report that schools are also good sources of information.

It is important that these people are familiar with the *Code of Practice*.

Training has been delivered to speech therapists in South Cheshire Health Trust and training is planned for the New Year for school nurses, health visitors and physiotherapists from the same Trust. More training will be offered in the year 1996/97. SENCO's will receive training at half-day conferences.

Issues

Parent partnership officers need to be conscious of the following issues:

1. Making schemes that are developed e.g. information packs, videos, support, available to any parent in the LEA that we work. This necessitates working with other partners who have access to parents.

2. Developing schemes of information and support that are sustainable after GEST funding disappears. We have tried to involve other partners and to hand over ownership of schemes to the partners.

3. We have needed to be conscientious about keeping in touch with parents and giving them the opportunity to steer parent partnership schemes. We have done this by arranging regular small meetings with parents.

4. Throughout the life of parent partnership schemes, it has been important to try to evaluate the effectiveness of our work. Since most of the work is developmental, the fruits of our labours will not be seen for some time, but parents have been able to tell us if we are moving in the right direction.

5 - Parents in Partnership
Geoff Lewis (Parent)

I hope today to be able to offer you a view of partnership in education and Stages 1 to 3 of the *Code of Practice* (see page 47), not only from the view of a parent but as a governor with special needs responsibility and as a voluntary worker with an organisation which aims to help, support, advise and provide practical information for anyone requiring it about developmental dyspraxia.

Wearing my hat as a governor for a moment, the special needs responsibility came about in 1988, ahead of the recommendations under the *Code of Practice*, through a pilot scheme in Cheshire.

When, some years later, it became obvious that my own son had difficulties I thought I was fairly well prepared for the statementing procedure. He was eventually statemented but it took two-and-a-half years to achieve.

At the time that sort of time span was not uncommon being before the *Code of Practice* was introduced.

The point I am making is that despite having some 'inside' knowledge this was of little advantage to me. What then was the chance of those without who did not have access to the same information?

The legacy left behind from the old system can mean that parents still see the statementing procedure as being long and drawn out.

Parents who contact us at the voluntary group have been known to describe the process of statementing assessment by comparing it to a long journey through a dark tunnel, with no light at the end and with no one to guide them. They are given no map and are not furnished with a torch or a lamp to show the way.

Others have compared the news of their child having a disability with being told they have a mountain to climb.

The problem being that not only do they have to climb the mountain but they have to find out its name, find out which country it is in and then locate it, before they can even begin the climb.

Parents are wrestling with coming-to-terms with their child's problems as well as starting on the statementing process. Surely the easier this process can be made the better.

Parents often feel blinded by jargon and 'Education Speak' and sometimes feel that their views on THEIR child are not given the credence they should be; after all if partnership is to work parents would seem to me to be key members of the team as they after all are the experts when it comes to their own children.

Working as part of an organisation which gives one-to-one help to parents and many others gives an insight and overview of the statementing procedures. In relation to Stages 1 to 3 contact with parents who write or telephone for advice constantly makes me ask the question 'Whatever happened to Stages 1 and 2?'

The majority of parents contact us with **no** knowledge of parent partnership, **no** knowledge of expressions of concern or of the stages of assessment. When discussing individual cases over the phone we find many have already reached Stage 3. This is often with no previous contact or consultation with the school.

We have in the past been contacted by schools requiring information about the disability. Having given the information requested we have then been told that it was to enable them to give an appropriate request for Stage 4 formal assessment. When we have asked about parental involvement we have, on occasions, been told that they have not been told yet. Whilst I would accept that this is not the case in all schools, it does happen and it is worrying.

It is imperative that all who have any dealings with the requirements and recommendations made within the *Code of Practice* should have a full and clear understanding of their role and responsibilities.

Partnership is now establishing a way forward in many areas. There is no reason why parents in partnership should not achieve its objectives, setting out to reduce conflict, obstructions, misunderstandings and a reduction of the number of cases going to tribunal. Partnership can succeed if parents are accepted as equals in the process. The days when parents were seen as having to be pacified or fobbed off are surely gone.

The key word today should be **information**. Informing parents and keeping them informed, a willingness to share information, accepting information from parents about their child is or should be all part of the process. After all, parents can often be the best people to find out details from.

Information exchange by discussion is vital in the initial stages of the statementing procedure, but this needs to start at Stage 1.

Schools, parents, voluntary groups, education, health and in some cases social services have to have avenues to exchange views, reports and information. The parent partnership initiative is one way in which parents and voluntary groups can help smooth out the wrinkles.

There are however problems. Whilst Special Needs Co-ordinators in our schools have very limited non-contact time (if any) in order to deal with their responsibilities and the parent partnership initiative funding is set to end in 1997, one wonders if any of it will ever work.

The concept of the Named Person Scheme is good but not in my view particularly well thought out. Whilst many parent partnership officers practise mouth to mouth resuscitation and others are still trying to kick start the whole process, many voluntary organisations are stepping back from taking named person responsibility on board but are carrying on doing what they have always done, giving help, advice and information.

The Named Person Scheme is patchy the whole country over. Parents need this service and some uniformity is necessary.

At the moment the quality of the product depends upon where you live and what sort of training the named person has been given, if any.

It is vital that parents are kept informed, helped and assisted. This enables them to make informed decisions and contribute to the whole process of assessment and statementing as it was intended.

I cannot see why partnership with good exchange of information between parents, the statutory authorities and the voluntary sector cannot provide the hand lamp to guide parents through the long dark tunnel and to help them not only identify and find their mountain but also guide them on their path towards the summit.

The parent partnership initiative is the vehicle which can develop this mediation service to benefit all those involved in special needs education.

6 - 'Telling it as it is' - a SENCO's View (1)
Lesley Burrell (Primary School Teacher)

I was asked by a Parent Partnership Officer, Linda Caldecott, to speak at NASEN's conference at Haydock Park in November 1995 as a SENCO (Special Educational Needs Co-ordinator) and to 'tell it as it is!'. My first reaction was panic. The thought of speaking to those people terrified me but I decided that I could strike a blow for overworked SENCO's everywhere, so in trepidation I agreed. To cut a long story short I have briefly outlined the content below.

My school is a largish split-site, primary school in Warrington with 385 on the roll. We are also one of two schools in Warrington designated to accept physically handicapped children. We have 42 children presently on our SEN register.

My role within the school is as follows:
- SENCO;
- class teacher for 29 Y3 children;
- music co-ordinator (with Christmas *and* OFSTED coming!);
- leader teacher for lower junior department;
- teacher representative in Governing body;
- a teachers' union representative;
- history co-ordinator until September 1995. The job was then allocated to a colleague;
- and oh yes, a wife, mother in my spare time!

This means I have some level of responsibility for 71 children. That is also 71 sets of parents who need some support and, of them, 42 sets of parents with big worries.

To be told 'your child has special educational needs' is a real blow to parents. They desperately want their child to be the same as everybody else's. They do not want them to be different. The news is delivered and it is a shock. There seems to be an element of blame, failure and certainly bewilderment especially where the *Code of Practice* is concerned. These parents really fear for their child's future. What now? What will happen? Will he/she have to go to a special school? Some parents panic and buy WH Smith's workbooks and engage a tutor in the hope their child will catch up!

Who is in the front line to help and knows the child and possibly the parents? - the SENCO. I issue an A4 leaflet explaining the stages their child may or may not go through when they are told 'the news'. We need to form a relationship based on knowledge and trust. This will develop if parents are informed and kept up-to-date, invited to IEP (Individual Education Plan) meetings and reviews and are made to feel part of the decision making process. **They know their child!** When uninformed parents become informed through scratching around for information they can be very bitter and rightly so. If all this was observed maybe the money kept back for tribunals could be spent on provision - a simplistic view I know. I am sure that imagination is probably much worse than knowing the facts.

The real issue for me is **time!**

I need time to: support parents, hold reviews; liaise with staff (how is Johnny doing?); liaise with learning support staff; liaise with occupational therapists and physiotherapists; ring parents to ask them to arrange an opthoptist appointment; arrange special language assessments; speak to the educational psychologists; see the English as a second language staff; help write IEPs and so on. I have had Friday afternoons since September as non-contact time to try to fulfil this role as long as the headteacher is available to have my class. All this will lead to **overload.** I feel there is a mistake just waiting to happen. Something waiting to be forgotten. It is difficult to fulfil all my roles within the school well.

A special educational needs development officer visited school. He needed to see a statement on a child. It was in my filing cabinet. The officer arrives in my classroom just as I am helping a child.

For example:

Alice with the mysteries of tens and units and I have just noticed Robert gazing into space. I am not sure which planet he was on but it was not earth! I find the statement, leaving my file on the table, and we try to discuss this child while what seemed like the Battle of Waterloo raged around us. Alice is tugging at my clothes 'You said ....' Robert is still in outer space. I eventually speak to the class about being mature enough to carry on with work and not to be noisy. The outcome was that I did not feel that I had fought the statemented child's case very well, I had not taught Alice how to add tens and units and when I asked Robert where his work was he smiled sweetly and said, 'Under your file!' Then it was lunch time, PE, music, story - and

Alice and I had to start all over again the next day.

Another example was trying to ring the educational psychologist. If you ring at lunch time, not unreasonably she is out to lunch! When she rings back in the afternoon, I am with my class. I need to speak to her urgently, so have to leave the class, gabble my message and return three minutes later to find that Adam has pushed Michelle into the book bag box! There is usually some interruption to my class every week and the children are entitled to 100 per cent of my attention.

I applauded the introduction of the *Code of Practice*. Even I could see we needed a uniform approach to SEN but it should have come with lots and lots of money. The implications for my school, if I was to have more time to do my SENCO role, would be 35+ in each class and mixed ages and key stages. It seems to me that any 'good idea' in education is at the expense of something else. The job does get done successfully **so far**!

Any parent partnership scheme would help alleviate the burden on SENCOs. Some parents are happy to join support groups or even start them. Some parents want their child's problems with a professional and these are the parents who need the support to alleviate the feelings of guilt, failure and confusion which very often go with special educational needs. The SENCO could have the information and point the way!

My closing plea to the conference is for the *Code of Practice* to be properly financed! We can live in hope!

The West Sussex Experience
7 - Parental Involvement in the *Code of Practice*: Stages 1 to 3
Lindsay Haines (Parent Partnership Officer)

1994 saw the appointment of parent partnership officers in many LEAs (Local Education Authorities). Funding for these posts is provided through GEST (Grants for Education Support and Training) and LEA funding. Many parent partnership schemes are about to enter their third and possibly final year of funding under the GEST scheme. Parent partnership schemes were established to support the implementation of the *Code of Practice* and, within our scheme in West Sussex, it was envisaged that the focus of the work would be Stages 4 and 5 as identified in the *Code of Practice* (see page 47). In West Sussex we have focused on the following areas:

- to provide advice and support to parents on general matters relating to statutory assessments, statements and right of appeal;
- to assist in the identification of people willing to be named persons;
- to bring together representatives of voluntary organisations and the LEA on a regular basis to discuss the development of special needs provision in the county;
- to investigate the information and support needs of parents and voluntary agencies and assist with the identification of priorities for improvement;
- to collaborate with voluntary organisations in providing training opportunities for parents, organisations and named persons;
- to seek out parental views on the quality of the service provided during the statutory assessment and identify areas for improvement.

So how has the West Sussex parent partnership scheme become involved with the Stages 1 to 3? I believe the key words are 'information' and 'communication'.

Advice and support to parents

There is a leaflet advertising a telephone service to parents and it is used by parents seeking a diverse range of advice including parents with children at Stages 1 to 3. Many calls in this latter category fall into two main groups: Firstly, from parents of pre-school children approaching school entry who do not understand how the *Code of Practice* applies to them; secondly, from parents with school-aged children who are experiencing some difficulty in their relationship with the school.

To support the parents of pre-school children, I attend two pre-school centres each term to talk with parents and answer their questions. In parts of the county where we do not have such centres, I know that playgroups, opportunity groups and the Portage service will suggest to parents that they can contact me. Recent work has been undertaken by our educational psychology service to produce a booklet for parents of pre-school children who may have special needs.

The main focus of my support to parents of school aged children is to explain the SEN stages, clarify the parents' own information needs because information is often what they want and then encourage the parent to discuss their concerns with the relevant professional. Parents often do not understand the concept of a continuum of provision and still see a statement as the goal they must strive for. The parents of children at Stages 2 and 3 may only see their child receiving, in their opinion, the minimum of support. I have spoken to parents who talk about their child receiving extra help from a teacher who may turn out to be a parent volunteer of NTA (non-teaching assistant). Or conversely suggest that it is a parent helping their child who may be a non-teaching assistant specifically funded to support a prepared programme of work. Parents may not know what SEN stage their child is on or have heard of an IEP let alone have been involved in the development of that plan.

We may feel that Stage 4 involves a lot of paperwork and terminology for parents to cope with, but it does come with written information, a time-scale and the option to have a named person. Parents at Stages 1 to 3 also need information, they also need some indication of time and more fundamentally have the right to know what level of support or need their child has. So if, in West Sussex, a parent comes to speak to a teacher or SENCO again with more questions, it may be the fault of the parent partnership officer, but I hope that the information I give to parents enables them to ask specific and relevant questions, which in turn provide them with the information they require to be a positive and active partner in their child's education. I hope that the communication which takes place assists the teacher or SENCO to clarify the parents' particular concern and in the end may also save them time.

Communication

In West Sussex, we have established a Special Educational Needs Forum to enable regular dialogue between LEA officers, county councillors and voluntary organisations. It provides an opportunity for the LEA to update the voluntary groups on developments and proposals for change and seeks their views. Within the Forum, we have formed sub-groups to look at topics which are important to us all. Already we are beginning to review written information together to see if we can make the content more user-friendly and to suggest different levels of written information. One valuable idea that we hope to put into practice in the coming year is to provide a number of open evenings throughout the county which parents will be able to attend and have the opportunity to speak to a wide range of professionals and representatives of voluntary organisations.

I have begun to plan a day suggested by our named persons at a recent meeting. They feel that they would benefit from a refresher training day and I hope we will be able to run a day in the early autumn focusing on our work within the *Code of Practice*. That is how the system works and how professions contribute to the process of supporting and assessing children's needs. The named persons also want to know more about the voluntary organisations and the support they offer. Developing from the original idea of training for named persons, I hope that we will also open the day to parents.

Finally, another form of communication is the parent partnership newsletter. It was not planned, it evolved and is now circulated to all schools, voluntary organisations and relevant professionals in health, social services and education. The present edition contained a list of all our voluntary groups in the county involved in special educational needs which, it is hoped, will assist schools in providing information to parents on relevant groups as recommended in the *Code of Practice*. The newsletter also provides calendar information on meetings, talks and events. It encourages readers to contribute articles and each edition will focus on a particular aspect of development within the parent partnership scheme.

I believe that in the past year and half, the parent partnership scheme has been able to build on the relationships already established with the voluntary sector and parents in particular.

I hope in the coming year to be able to work more closely with schools in promoting an even greater sense of partnership with parents and hope that you agree that information and communication must continue to be the key words.

8 - 'What worked and what didn't'
Sue Coules (Parent)

My name is Sue and I am a mother of four. I am also a Portage home visitor and a local authority Named Person. My two middle children, James 13 and Richard 10, have special needs. Richard has ADD (Attention Deficit Disorder), dyslexia and Tourettes syndrome and has been prescribed the drugs Ritalin and Clonidene. Richard has moved from one middle school to another middle school. I moved him as I felt he needed a more sympathetic atmosphere. He is at Stage 2 and this means he receives a little extra help within the school. This comes in many forms. A teacher who understands his problems, the whole school which has a reward system of stars, certificates, praise by the headteacher. At the moment this appears to be working although Richard does have bad days as well as good but the school and I take them as they come. The school has not been difficult about Richard's medication and all the staff are very approachable. This is a big help. A parent who has a child on the SEN stages needs to feel staff are there to help. What has worked for Richard is getting extra help, staff who are approachable and the involvement of the whole school. There does not seem to have been anything which has not worked for Richard. Being able to change his school was a plus not a minus. It gave me confidence in the system because I was allowed to exercise my rights.

James is 13½ and has ADHD (Attention Deficit and Hyperactivity Disorder). Just to clarify one small point. A child with ADD tends to be passive and compliant as opposed to one with ADHD who behaves like a demented maniac. James is no longer in the school system. I removed him prior to half-term. His removal is in no way a reflection on the school that he was attending. They did everything in their power to educate my son but unfortunately he found the classroom situation intolerable. He was at SEN Stage 3.

The SENCO correctly identified my son's problems within three weeks of him starting and she and her department worked tirelessly to help James. I have no problem with either of my children's schools nor with the SEN department.

It is not really the system that has in James' case or will in Richard's case let them down. It really is a problem of finances and resources that is preventing my children from receiving the education that is their right. This is not just a local problem or a national problem it is a global fault. There is not a country in the world that has money to burn and I accept that. It is just a real shame that my children will be left wanting.

9 - 'Telling it as it is' - A SENCO's view (2)
Sarah Searle-Barnes (Primary School Teacher)

I was asked to 'tell it how it is' on behalf of SENCOs. As we have already heard, we are working as partners for the best interests of our children and it is as well for others to understand the pressures their partners are under. In my experience the job of SENCO is not particularly oversubscribed. It appears to be more vocational than a good career move. The teaching profession as a whole is struggling with overload and SENCOs in particular.

I trained in special education and taught in a school for severe learning difficulties for four years and then in a school for children with physical disabilities. I then had a break to have three children and am married to a GP in Worthing. I was enticed back to teaching by a friend who was a headmaster and has a Downs Syndrome child in mainstream who needed teaching support. I am still teaching at that school and I have a Y2 class as well as being SENCO.

Under the present school organisation there are three days for special needs allocated out of the school budget. A colleague of mine takes two days for Stage 2 teaching support and I take one day - euphemistically described as my 'day off'.

To put 'liaising with parents' in context, I thought it might be helpful to look at my job description which is at the end of this article. During the rest of my week I have a Y2 class - 31 children - with the usual responsibilities of a class teacher.

The liaison with parents is a crucial part of my role and perhaps the one that takes the most time. The *Code* put into print what every good teacher has always known that the role of the parent in the education of their child is crucial. Teachers come and go but the parent is always there, perhaps most importantly at the point of leaving the school system and entering the world outside.

One of the most difficult aspects of my job with parents is enabling them to come to terms with the difficulties their child has. One of the main advantages of the *Code* is the proposed cycle of support given over a period of months or years. This means that there are successive meetings with parents talking through targeted teaching to meet their child's needs and meetings to review the child's progress in response to that teaching. This enables a partnership of trust and mutual support to be gradually built up. If progress has to made through to Stages 4 and 5 we are building on that ongoing relationship which must be for the good of the child. It has been my privilege to work alongside some extremely dedicated and yet pragmatic parents who are determined that their child should be given the opportunity to achieve and be happy at their own level of academic ability. There have been speakers this morning who have talked about 'passion' and the way in which parents can present their child's case with conviction. This is of course true - as a parent myself I understand that - but I would warn against reading a professional appearance of objectivity as disinterest. Teachers do care about the children in their charge and often become very involved with children experiencing failure. Occasionally parents are disappointed and seek to blame systems, teachers, each other or even the child. This is much more difficult to work through. The 'myth' of catching up either with extra tuition or by a change of teacher or school can be very debilitating for the child. This kind of situation is stressful for the parent, the teachers and above all the child. With the support of parents and good teaching the child should above all else develop the famous 'feel good factor' and discover other areas of the curriculum, such as art or PE in which to excel. The developments in information technology also create great opportunities for academic success previously denied special needs children.

My main pressure points

- *Time* - I am extremely fortunate in having a very supportive head and governing body who until now have been able to fund special needs adequately. Other SENCOs are not so fortunate. I have Fridays out of class - supposedly my 'day off', but it keeps my head above water - just. I am very conscious that with impending budgetary cuts special needs is an expensive area involving relatively few children. This can be a pressure in the staff room with budgetary bids for high profile curriculum areas.

- *Availability* - I am very conscious of the price paid by my class of six year olds who actually have to be trained each September to cope with a much higher than average number of interruptions and messages coming in and out of the classroom. It is definitely worth booking 'high quality' time to talk with teachers - it is never particularly positive from the teachers point of view to have parents turn up at 3.15pm expecting 'in-depth' consultations on their child. Home note books are a good and proven form of liaison between home and school and can encourage the child to take responsibility for communication and avoid the 'does he take sugar?' syndrome developing.

- *Expectations* - We live in a society where the expectations of the consumer - speaking from personal experience of my husband's patients as well as parents, are extremely high and encouraged to be high. There can be conflict when dealing with parents and other professionals who are involved with one particular 'special' child - teachers are involved with that child but always in the context of the needs of 30 other children which is a somewhat different ball game but, perhaps, it is a good preparation for real life.

As with all new legislation, the *Code of Practice* needs to be worked through and the wrinkles ironed out. West Sussex with its 'Key

Routes' system has enabled us to be one step ahead of the basic requirements. Parents and teachers working in partnership is good news for any child and an area which is rightly highlighted in the *Code*. One hopes the resources to meet that expectation will be forthcoming and sustained.

SENCO's job description

- co-ordinating the management of individual children's special education provision;
- collation of Key Routes material;
- giving support to class teachers in use of Key Routes procedures;
- liaising with the parents who have children with special educational needs;
- liaising between class teachers, literacy tutors, behavioural advice, occupational therapy advice, speech therapy advice, as appropriate for individual children;
- formulating and monitoring of Individual Education Plans for children on Stages 2 to 5, in liaison with staff concerned;
- co-ordinating the non-teaching assistant support available to special needs;
- providing resources to facilitate coping with the specific needs of individual children;
- working with the educational psychologist on assessments of individual needs;
- co-ordinating the screening process in reading and early years;
- compiling and reviewing every six months the register of children with identified special needs;
- using diagnostic materials with individual children where appropriate;
- co-ordinating the annual reviews for statemented children.

10 - 'What worked and what didn't'
Barbara Hogan (Named Person)

I have been a Named Person volunteer for just over a year and have helped two families.

My role is to assist and support parents during the statementing of their child, for example, helping them complete forms in their own words, attend meetings if necessary and most importantly just to listen. I am not there to make or tell them how to make decision. The two families were completely different and posed different problems. The first family had a six year old boy who had severe speech, learning and behavioural problems and was being statemented through the usual channels, that is the school.

The mother felt that she too had language problems and as a result had had problems with her son's school resulting in a lack of communication on both sides.

She also felt that the school was not always sympathetic to her son's problems and considered him to be disruptive. This made her feel that she was on her own. There was also a three year old brother who also had speech and learning difficulties.

In this particular case, I felt that the mother looked on me as an ordinary person to whom she could talk easily. Her son was eventually statemented and accepted into a speech and language unit, much to the delight of the mother. This gave her confidence to deal with her younger son's problems before he started school.

The other family had a 15 year old asthmatic girl whose school and doctor had managed and coped well. However, the mother felt that, as her daughter spent much of last year in the medical room rather than in class, her daughter would benefit by going to a special school for asthmatics so that she would be able to take her GCSEs, as well as her illness being catered for.

The mother had written letters to different people in education so she herself had set the statutory assessment process in motion, rather than the school. Because of this, the mother wanted reassurance from me that she was not wrong in doing this and also to explain that apart from the educational aspect she also wanted her daughter to take her exams at the same age as ordinary children, also for her to have the chance to mix with other children as she was becoming extremely isolated by her illness.

I only visited her once, but she rang on several occasions for reassurance. During one particular conversation she asked if it would be acceptable if she sent a poem that her daughter had written about her feelings to the education authority. She felt that her daughter was of the age where her own thoughts should be considered.

The advantage of a Named Person volunteer for the parent is that we are ordinary people to whom they can talk freely about any problems and if necessary pass on any fears or problems they may have. Also that they can trust us.

For myself the pleasure of being a volunteer is knowing that just by being there and listening you have helped a family.

11 - What parents need to know
Katy Simmons (IPSEA)

IPSEA (the Independent Panel for Special Education Advice) is a national charity that gives advice and support to parents of children with special educational needs. We are also the only national charity attempting to provide free representation at SEN Tribunals for parents with children with special educational needs, whatever the nature of their learning difficulty/disability and regardless of the school placement being sought by their parents. The contents of this article are based on my experience as an IPSEA volunteer and later, as an IPSEA worker.

When parents seek advice from the voluntary sector they have often reached the end of the road and are facing problems which cannot be resolved through partnership. Research carried out by IPSEA in 1992 and again in 1995 showed that when parents sought help, many described themselves as being 'at a dead end'. On each occasion, the research showed that at the time parents made contact with IPSEA, in one in five cases, children were already out of school, withdrawn by the parents because of disputes over provision.

In such circumstances, what do parents need to know? On one level, the *1993 Education Act*, which came into effect on September 1, 1994, should have put an end to many of their problems. Described by Baroness Blatch as 'a new framework for special education provision', it introduced time limits on assessments and established an appeal system that gave parents many more opportunities to challenge LEA decisions. IPSEA's research showed that parental frustrations with lengthy assessments had, by 1994, become virtually a thing of the past. However the new Act had created new needs, the implications of which are only now beginning to be felt by the voluntary sector.

The new appeal system

The special educational needs tribunal, created by the new *Act*, replaced an appeal system that was clearly unfair and inadequate. Under the *1981 Act*, parents had rights of appeal to local appeal panels, set up by the same LEA that had made the disputed decision. Even if the parents' appeal was successful, these panels only had limited power to remit the case back to the LEA for reconsideration. After such reconsideration, LEAs could decide to uphold their original decision, at which point the parents' only option was to appeal to the Secretary of State for Education, a process that could and often did take years. Not surprisingly, few parents used the appeal system.

On September 1, 1994 all this changed. The *1993 Act* gave parents a greatly increased number of occasions on which they could appeal against an LEA decision and established an independent Tribunal, under the auspices of the Council on Tribunals, which was empowered to make final and binding decisions.

The number of appeals in the first few months astonished the secretariat of the new Tribunal: in the year that has followed there is no sign that take-up of appeal rights will diminish. New appeal rights, while on one level empowering parents have, however, created a new set of needs. Parents' new needs now focus on two specific areas - evidence and representation. Access to both is essential if a parental appeal is to have a chance of success.

Evidence

The President of the Special Educational Needs Tribunal, Trevor Aldridge QC, made it clear from the outset that the remit of the tribunal was not to consider history, but to look at the child's needs 'on the day of the tribunal'. The emphasis from the start has been on evidence and evidence of the most up-to-date kind.

LEAs naturally have immediate access to this kind of information. They can, and do, send their professionals into school the day before a hearing. Unfortunately, as the employers of most of the people who have the most regular contact with the child, they can, and in some LEAs routinely do, exert an influence on the nature of the data that is collected. Evidence given to the House of Commons select committee by a number of voluntary agencies showed that pressure on professionals is a serious concern. Recent research by IPSEA has shown the extent of this problem. Professionals are often reluctant to give evidence on a parent's behalf and may be 'warned off' by the LEA if they try to do so.

For parents with sufficient means, the obvious solution to this problem is an independent second opinion. But the sheer cost of such evidence puts it beyond the means of many.

So for many, the first problem is 'What evidence can I use and who will give it?'

Representation

The next main hurdle for parents is the presentation of their case and the hearing itself. Although the process is meant to be 'parent friendly' and most parents speak positively of their experiences of the staff at the Tribunal, the fact remains that the tribunal process is part of the judicial system. IPSEA's recent research has shown that, for even the most able and articulate parents, the process itself, not to mention the hearing, are intimidating and daunting experiences.

Only parents with the lowest incomes are eligible for Legal Aid to prepare their case. There is no Legal Aid for representation at hearings and the average cost of solicitor representation is at least £1,000. Further, there is no evidence that representation by a solicitor is helpful for parents, since it tends to lead to more legalistic hearings which do not necessarily produce the desired outcome.

So, for many parents the next problem is, 'Where should I go to find help and support when beginning an appeal?'

What do parents need to know in order to answer these questions?

The legal framework

Parents need to be aware that the law entitles children to have their needs identified, assessed and met with regularly reviewed provision and that these entitlements are set out in the *1993 Education Act* and in the *1994 Education (Special Educational Needs) Regulations*.

As part of the assessment process, the LEA seeks evidence (advice) from a number of sources and has statutory duties relating to the nature of that advice it collects. Of central importance is Regulation 6(2) of the *1994 Education (Special Educational Needs) Regulations*, where the statutory obligation of LEAs in relation to the content of advice is clearly set out.

This regulation gives clear emphasis, not only to the setting out of the child's needs, but to the obligation of the LEA to require the professional involved to comment on the provision that the child needs.

When drawing up the statement, the LEA will ultimately be required, under S168(2)(b) of the *1993 Education Act*, to specify the special educational provision to be made for the child. The *Code of Practice* goes further (section 4:8) in saying that the provision should be quantified.

While one might argue that it is the LEA that has these duties, not the advice giver, it is surely in the interests of all if the advice giver, aware of what will be required of the LEA at a later point, furnishes the detail which will enable the LEA to meet its legal duty. The advice giver is not prescribing provision: it is after all, 'only advice', which the LEA, as advice gatherer must then sift through in order to make decisions.

Advice givers, IPSEA would argue, cannot write advice without giving due consideration to the broader legal framework in which they are working, which imposes legal obligations on their employers and guarantees entitlement of provision for their clients. In IPSEA's experience of advising parents, appeals often arise directly from situations where the statement, based on advice which does not offer details of provision required by the child, in its turn does not spell out the provision the child should have.

On a simple practical level, if advice givers do not give details of provision in their advice, then by use of the summons, parents can require them to do so at a Tribunal, possibly under oath. Giving details of required provision at the outset may ultimately mean that such confrontational situations are avoided, since once parents have fuller information, they may be more satisfied with what is on offer. Inadequate parental access to information is likely to trigger tribunal cases and litigation.

Parents should be aware of the 1995 House of Lords ruling on the duty of care. This ruling was made in relation to a number of cases (E v Dorset; Christmas v Hampshire; Keating v Bromley) where parents of children with special educational needs were seeking to claim damages for negligence on the part of the LEAs. The judges ruled that individual professionals could be liable if they failed to exercise care and 'reasonable skills' in relation to children with special educational needs. As a result of this judgement, professionals, and the LEAs who as employers are vicariously responsible for them, could find themselves being sued by parents. It could be argued that advice givers who do not provide as much detail as possible about how a child's needs might be met might lay themselves and their LEAs open to challenge by parents in the future on the grounds that their advice has been negligent.

Parents therefore need to be aware of the legal context in which advice givers are writing and of the legal duties that LEAs have in relation to that advice. If advice was written as the law intends, then not only would appeals be likely to be reduced, but the problems parents face in relation to evidence would be reduced. Detailed advice would enable all parents, not simply those who could afford to pay for a second opinion, to decide whether the provision on offer met their child's needs.

The challenges of representation

There have already been charges levelled that more articulate and privileged parents are using the new Tribunal system to take an unfair share of limited resources. Given the newness of the system and the stressful nature of appeal, it is hardly surprising that it is the more confident and educated parents who have, so far, used the process with most energy.

However, the big question now facing the voluntary sector is how to help less articulate and confident parents to gain access to Tribunal decisions. While some voluntary organisations have seen the need and are developing parental advocacy services to support parents at Tribunals, not all have taken on the challenges of the new system. There are a number of reasons for their reluctance to take on Tribunal work. It is undoubtedly stressful and demanding, involving close reading of the documents and awareness of the law. It often involves conflict with decision makers and long-term commitment to cases which may go on long after the hearing. It is expensive in terms of time and effort: representatives need proper indemnity and on-going support.

But for the new system to succeed it is essential that the voluntary sector takes on the challenge, so that no parent who is unwilling to do so should go unrepresented to the Tribunal.

Summary

In 1992, the Audit Commission pointed out that parents supported either by a lawyer or by the voluntary sector tended to be more satisfied than others who were unsupported. The new law has not changed that situation.

So what do parents need to ensure that **all** children with special educational needs have access to the assessment and provision that is their legal entitlement?

They need **information** about that entitlement from independent people who understand the law and the legal framework within which LEAs should operate.

They need professionals - teachers, psychologists - who also understand those legal duties and their own place within the legal framework of special education and who write the kind of **detailed advice** that the law intends. They may need support from **volunteer** professionals who are willing to do independent assessments and to support parents at Tribunals where local advice, for whatever reason, is unsatisfactory.

They need increased support from the **voluntary sector** in order to understand the legal framework, pursue their child's entitlement effectively and where necessary exercise their right to appeal to the SEN Tribunal.

Parents need the kind of support that will turn legal entitlement into reality for all children with special educational needs.

12 - Partnership with parents: vision or reality?
Sheila Wolfendale, University of East London

Let me start by asking the reader whether you have a vision of what a really good home-school partnership is? If you do, what does it consist of? As partners, who would do what? How would you, as partners, act on behalf of children? What do you think are the rights and responsibilities that go with a partnership relationship?

When we look at some developments in the area of home-school links and working relations between professionals and parents, we may react differently according to whether we are parents, teachers, educational psychologists, etc.

Reminders of significant developments

Recent educational legislation (*1980, 1981, 1986, 1992* and *1993 Education Acts*) has encouraged parental rights and parents' charters have been proposed as a means of promoting 'the parents as consumer' concept. In fact, the OFSTED 'Framework for Inspection' sets out the requirements for inspectors to ascertain parents' views in their children's school(s) by sending out a questionnaire as well as by holding a parents meeting as part of the inspection process. The Framework for Inspection itself contains a number of 'performance indicators' on parental and community involvement by which schools can be judged and held accountable.

The basic premise is that involving parents and carers in education increases children's achievement.

A substantial literature now exists within the UK on parental partnership (e.g. Wolfendale, 1992, Bastiani and Wolfendale, 1996) which describes theory, research and applications.

Literature and research show, time and time again, that parental involvement is one of the key factors that contributes to school effectiveness.

The rationale on which home-school links have rested includes these assumptions:

- that parents are experts on their own children;
- that parental skills and expertise can be used hand-in-hand with teachers' knowledge and skills;

- that teachers' morale and output is enhanced by parental co-operation;
- that children benefit from home-school co-operation.

Innumerable projects have focused on parental/family involvement in reading and literacy (Wolfendale and Topping, 1996), in maths (Merttens and Vass, 1993), in assessment (Wolfendale, 1993), other curriculum areas and policy-making.

Special Educational Needs - setting the pace in partnership with parents?

The many innovations in this area, post-Warnock Report (1978) and *1981 Education Act* could lead us, reasonably, to conclude that this is a pace-setting area. The most notable and sustained example of parents and professionals working together on a basis of equality and sharing expertise is that of Portage; other examples of initiative during the 1980s was the formation, up and down the country, of parents' groups, acting both as lobbying and supporting parents.

Whereas the *1981 Education Act* provided a framework and impetus for improving the quality and amount of co-operative working, it took the advent of the *1993 Education Act* (Part 3) and its associated *Code of Practice* (1994) to extend and enhance parental rights in SEN assessment and decision-making and to provide a set of underpinning partnership values and principles (Beveridge, 1995). The Department of Education (and Employment, as it has been since Summer 1995) booklets for parents have explained their rights under the new *Act*, the *Code of Practice* and the new Tribunal System.

Aware of the need to resource such developments, the DFE included in the GEST (Grants for Education Support and Training) scheme for 1994-5, 1995-6 and 1996-7 grants to LEAs to set up and administer Parent-Partnership schemes. The vast majority of LEAs have appointed parent partnership officers, are developing named person provision and encouraging local and voluntary groups to pursue partnership objectives. Early signs are encouraging - local schemes report the development of productive relationships with parents; information and materials for parents; formation of parents' groups. A national Parent Partnership Network has been created and is based at the Council for Disabled Children (see references and Appendix 4).

So much achieved, so much more to achieve

There is much to celebrate in the area of parent-professional relations, but we are reminded that there are still many parents/families who do not experience such productive and constructive relations. Some parent-writers, such as Gascoigne (1995) highlight basic differences between the remit and concerns of parents and professionals, and, whilst not ruling out the potential for partnership, emphasise how much ground work needs to be undertaken before constructive co-working can take place.

Models of partnership in the area of SEN continue to abound (Wolfendale 1992, Hornby 1995, Dale 1995) each of which provides a useful framework for negotiation.

But whilst attitudes are changing, facilitated in part by the legislation, resources and provision still lag behind as a recent survey confirms. In *Expert Opinions* (Beresford 1995), the views of over a thousand parents of children with severe disabilities were canvassed. Amongst the findings are the facts that: half the parents sampled described their relationship with professionals as positive and supportive; one in three parents belonged to a support group; one third of the sample said they felt poorly informed about services.

These and other statistics presented in the report confirm progress and clearly highlight continuing problem-areas within parental access to information, supportive provision and family friendly service delivery.

NASEN has responded to these challenges by adopting a policy for *Partnership with Parents*, integral to which is a commitment to attract more parent members. If this succeeds, a remarkable coalition could evolve whereby the largest SEN organisation, which has hitherto catered mainly for teachers, embraces parents as natural partners in an alliance for children.

13 - References and further reading

Andrews, E (1992) *An evaluation of the work of IPSEA*, IPSEA.

Andrews, E (1996) *Representing Parents at the SEN Tribunal*, IPSEA.

Bastiani, J and Wolfendale, S (eds.) *Home-School work in Britain: review, reflection and development*, David Fulton Publishers: London.

Beresford, B (1995) *Expert Opinions, a national survey of parents caring for a severely disabled child*, The Policy Press: Bristol University.

Beveridge, S (1995) Patterns of Partnership, *Special!*, Issue 4.3, Autumn.

Dale, N (1995) *Working with Parents of Children with Special Educational Needs*, Cassell: London.

Hornby, G (1995) *Working with Parents of Children with Special Educational Needs*, Cassell: London.

Gascoigne, E (1995) *Working with Parents as Partners in SEN*, David Fulton Publishers: London.

Merttens, R and Vass, J (1993) *Partnership in Maths: Parents and Schools*, Falmer Press: Lewes.

National Parent Partnership Network, Council for Disabled Children, at the National Children's Bureau, 8 Wakley Street, London EC1V 7QE.

Simmons, K (1992) *An evaluation of the work of IPSEA*, Oxford Polytechnic.

Special Educational Needs: the working of the Code of Practice and the Tribunal. Education Committee. Session 1995-96. Report together with the proceedings of the Committee, Minutes of Evidence and Appendices, HMSO: London.

Wolfendale, S (1992) *Empowering Parents and Teachers - working for Children*, Cassell: London.

Wolfendale, S (ed) (1993) *Assessing Special Educational Needs*, Cassell: London.

Wolfendale, S and Topping, K (eds.) (1996) *Family Involvement in Literacy - Effective Partnerships in Education*, Cassell: London.

Wolfendale, S (ed) (1997) *Working with Parents after the Code of Practice*, David Fulton Publishers: London.

Appendix 1 - Glossary of Terms

Attention Deficit Disorder (ADD) Short attention/concentration span.

Attention Deficit and Hyperactivity Disorder (ADHD) Very short attention/concentration span and hyperactive, often showing itself in the form of disruptive behaviour.

Clonidene A drug used in the treatment of ADHD.

Code of Practice Published in 1994, it is intended to be a guide to Local Education Authorities about the help they can offer to children with special educational needs.

Contact a Family A charity which encourages 'runaways' to contact their families to let them know they are safe. The charity has support groups for the families of young runaways.

Council of Tribunals The organisation responsible for administering the SEN Tribunal system.

Developmental Dyspraxia A specific learning difficulty, dyspraxic children are often labelled 'clumsy' as they have difficulty co-ordinating and controlling their movements.

Dyslexia A specific learning difficulty. According to the *1994 Code of Practice,* children who are dyslexic have 'significant difficulties in reading, writing, spelling and manipulating numbers, which are not typical for their general level of performance'.

EBD Emotional and behavioural difficulties.

GEST	Grants for Education Support and Training, provided by the government, for example, to fund the parent partnership initiative for the three years, 1994-95, 1995-96, 1996-97.
Individual Education Plan (IEP)	Every child at Stage 2 (or above) of special needs, should have an individual plan, outlining their needs and the methods to be used at school, and at home, to try and meet those needs. IEPs should be reviewed and updated termly.
Local Education Authorities (LEAs)	Responsible for providing education and for making assessments and maintaining statements of special educational needs.
MLD	Moderate learning difficulties.
Named Person	An independent adviser to parents/carers of children with special educational needs can be a member of the parents' family, a friend or member of a voluntary organisation.
Non-teaching Assistant (NTA)	Classroom helper with no teaching qualifications, usually under the management of the class teacher.
OFSTED	The body responsible for the inspection and assessment of all state schools, both mainstream and special.
Portage Workers	Portage is a scheme in which professionals work with parents of young children with special needs on an early learning intervention programme.
Ritalin	A drug used in the treatment of ADHD.
SEN	Special Educational Needs.

SENCO	Special Educational Needs Co-Ordinators are found in every state school. They are responsible for co-ordinating special needs provision in schools. They maintain the special needs register.
SENJIT	Special Educational Needs Joint Initiative Training (based in London) offers training to professionals working with children with special educational needs.
SEN Tribunal	An independent panel responsible for settling matters of dispute between LEAs and parents/carers of children with special educational needs.
SEN Register	Maintained by SENCOs in each school, it is a list of all the children in that school who have any sort of special educational need.
Severe Learning Difficulties	Multiple and complex, physical and/or mental disabilities.
Stages 1-5	The **staged** approach to special educational needs was formally introduced with the *Code of Practice* in 1994. A child with special educational needs of any description should be placed at one of the stages:

Stage 1 - a concern about the child is expressed by the child's parent or teacher.

Stage 2 - the Class teacher will seek advice from the SENCO and notify him/her of the concern.

Stage 3 - outside agencies will be asked to see the child and offer advice to the school about the best way to work with the child.

Stage 4 - a formal statutory assessment of the child's special educational needs is deemed necessary. This will usually include advice being sought from an educational psychologist and school doctor and will sometimes include a physiotherapist, speech therapist, and possibly social services.

Stage 5 - a decision to issue a statement of special educational needs is made in the light of very detailed information received from the formal assessment at Stage 4.

Tourettes Syndrome   An inherited disorder, manifesting in twitches, tics, involuntary uttering of noises.

Partnership with Parents in Action: Supporting NASEN Policy

Appendix 2 - Summary Table of the Legislation: The Education Act 1996

On 1 November 1996, the *1993 Education Act* was repealed. The law on special education was, from that date, contained in the *1996 Education Act*. This is a consolidating Act which pulls together among other Acts, the whole of the *1944 Education Act* and the *1993 Education Act*.

There have been no changes of substance to the law on special education, although recent amendments to the *1993 Act* made by the *Disability Discrimination Act 1995* and the *Nursery Education and Grant Maintained Schools Act* have been incorporated.

This 'translation table' is intended only as an aid to finding your way around the new law. As from 1 November, parent advisers will need to quote directly from, and refer to the sections in, the *1996 Act* itself.

Content	Before 1/11/96	After 1/11/96
The law on special educational needs.	Part lll, EA1993	Part lV, EA1996
Definitions of 'special educational needs' and 'special educational provision'.	Section 156	Section 312
Duty to 'have regard to' *Code of Practice*.	Section 157	Section 313
Issuing/revising the *Code of Practice*.	Section 158	Section 314
LEAs duty to review arrangements for special educational needs.	Section 159	Section 315
Duty to educate children with SEN in ordinary schools.	Section 160	Section 316
School governors' duties towards children with SEN.	Section 161 (1)-(5)	Section 317 (1)-(5)
Annual reports and arrangements for disabled pupils.	Section 29 (2) Disability Discrimination Act 1995	Section 317 (6) (7)
Provision of goods/services re SEN (4).	Section 162 (1) (2) (3)	Section 318 (1) (2)
Grants for nursery education.	Schedule 3, para 2, Nursery Education and Grant Maintained Schools Act 1996	Section 318 (3)

Content	Before 1/11/96	After 1/11/96
Provision 'otherwise' than in school.	Section 163	Section 319
Provision outside England and Wales.	Section 164	Section 320
Definition of children for whom LEAs are responsible.	Section 165	Section 321
Duty of Health Authority or local authority to help LEAs.	Section 166	Section 322 *change in terminology re local authority and health authority.*
Assessment.	Section 167	Section 323
Statement of Special Educational Needs.	Section 168	Section 324
Appeal against LEA refusal to issue Statement.	Section 169	Section 325
Appeal against contents of a Statement.	Section 170	Section 327
LEA access to schools.	Section 171	Section 327
Parental request for assessment of child with a Statement and right to appeal if LEA refuses.	Section 172 (1)-(5)	Section 328 (1)-(5)
Annual Review.	Section 172 (5)-(6)	Section 328 (5)-(6)
Parental request for assessment of a child with a Statement and a right to appeal if LEA refuses.	Section 173	Section 329

Content	Before 1/11/96	After 1/11/96
Governors' right to request assessment of a child with SEN.	Section 174	Section 330
Assessment of children under 2.	Section 175	Section 331
Health Authority duty to inform LEA of child with SEN.	Section 176	Section 332 *change in terminology re health authority*
Constitution of SEN Tribunal.	Section 177	Section 333
Membership of the SEN Tribunal.	Section 178	Section 334
Remuneration and expenses.	Section 179	Section 335
Tribunal procedure.	Section 180	Section 336
Making of assessments.	Schedule 9	Schedule 26
Making and maintenance of Statements.	Schedule 10	Schedule 27

Those sections of the **1994 Education Act** relating to making formal complaints against LEAs have been relocated as follows:

Complaints of LEAs acting unreasonably, Education Act 1996.	Section 68 EA1994	Schedule 496
Complaints of LEAs failing to fulfil their duty.	Section 99 EA1994	Schedule 497

Appendix 3 - NASEN's Policy Paper: Supporting Parents

Mission Statement

In order to foster its partnership aims NASEN will:

- recognise the primacy of the rights and interests of children and young people;
- provide a forum for the exchange of information between parents, professionals and other agencies;
- give appropriate support to parent members of NASEN;
- disseminate models of effective partnership practice both locally, nationally and internationally;
- monitor and report on the implementation of legislation in respect of children and young people with special educational needs and their families.

Parental Partnership in Practice
NASEN will seek to fulfil its aims and objectives with regard to parents and to those who are professionally involved with parents by:

1 Providing Information
1.1 introducing systematic procedures for dealing with telephone and written enquiries from parents and professionals;
1.2 having information leaflets for parents and professionals. These will include details of other contacts;
1.3 extending its database of information on parental partnership;
1.4 maintaining a small reference collection of information on parental partnership;
1.5 keeping up-to-date information on Parent Partnership Officers in LEAs and being an informed source about the ways in which they operate;
1.6 publishing articles and features about parental partnership in the *British Journal of Special Education, Support for Learning* and *Special!*;
1.7 publishing booklets and leaflets helpful to parents. These

measures will necessitate the allocation of appropriate funding and staffing.

2 *Professional Development*

2.1 training its paid staff and volunteers in effective ways of supporting both parents and professionals;

2.2 encouraging Branches to implement this policy through their meetings and other activities;

2.3 mounting courses which foster effective partnership with parents;

2.4 participating in the training of Parent Partnership Officers, when appropriate.

3 *Monitoring and Evaluation*

3.1 monitoring and evaluating this parental partnership policy;

3.2 monitoring developments nationally in respect of parents of children with special educational needs;

3.3 monitoring the implementation of legislation in respect of children with SEN and their families.

NASEN will seek to complement rather than duplicate the activities of other organisations which are already well established in the field.

Appendix 4 - SOURCES OF INFORMATION FOR PARENTS

ADD/ADHD Family Support Group UK
c/o Mrs G Mead, 1 a The High Street, Dilton Marsh, Westbury, Wilts., BA13 4DL, Tel: 01373 826045.
This group can offer a range of information and advice plus referral to a local self help group.

Advisory Centre for Education
1 b Aberdeen Studios, 22 Highbury Grove, London, N5 2EA, Tel: 0171 354 8321.
Publishes *Special Education Handbook* (which gives definitive account of the law on children with special educational needs). New edition due soon following 1996 Act. Essential reference material for all schools as well as parents. Also has telephone helpline each weekday afternoon.

Adult Dyslexia Organisation (ADO)
Donald Schloss, ADO, 336 Brixton Road, London, SW9 7AA, Tel: 0171 737 7646 (admin) or 0171 924 9559 (helpline), Fax: 0171 274 7840, e-mail: dyslexia;hq@dial.pipex.com.

Aids to Communication in Education (ACE)
ACE Centre, Ormerod School, Waynflete Road, Headington, Oxford, OX3 ODD, Tel: 01865 63508, Fax: 01865 750188, e-mail: acecent@dircor.co.uk
Provides a focus of information and expertise in the use of technology.

Association for Spina Bifida and Hydrocephalus (ASBAH)
Peter Walker, ASBAH House, 42 Park Road, Peterborough, PE1 2UQ, Tel: 01733 555988.
Offers advocacy service and support with reading papers, appeals and dealing with LEAs.

Association for All Speech Impaired Children (AFASIC)
347 Central Markets, London, EC1 9NH, Tel: 0171 236 3632/6487,
Fax: 0171 236 8115.
National organisation with network of local support groups for
parents.

British Association of Teachers of the Deaf (BATOD)
Mrs Ann Underwood, 41 The Orchard, Leven, Beverley, HU17
5QA, Tel/Fax: 01964 544243.

British Dyslexia Association (BDA)
98 London Road, Reading, RG1 5AU, Tel: 01734 662677,
Fax: 01734 351927,
e-mail - helpline: info@dyslexiahelp-bda.demon.co.uk
e-mail - admin@bda-dyslexia.demon.co.uk

BILD (British Institute of Learning Disabilities)
Wolverhampton Road, Kidderminster, Worcestershire, DY10 3PP,
Tel: 0156 285 0251, Fax: 01562 851 970.
Co-ordinates a large number of conferences, courses and
workshops. It also publishes a range of periodicals and books. Has
an Information and Resource Centre which answers enquiries and
provides a monthly bibliography as part of its Current Awareness
Service.

Centre for Studies in Inclusion in Education
1 Redland Close, Elm Lane, Redland, Bristol, BS6 6UE,
Tel: 0117 923 8450, Fax: 0117 923 8460.
Good source of free fact sheets on legislation, parents rights and
children's rights. Interesting materials on LEA practices and on
examples of good practice from schools. Campaigning for full
integration of all children into mainstream education before the year
2000.

Children's Legal Centre
University of Essex, Wivenhoe Park, Colchester, Essex, CO4 3SQ,
Tel: 01206 873820.
Gives free advice and information on legal questions.
Advice Line 10 - 12 noon; 2 - 5 pm.

Contact a Family
170 Tottenham Court Road, London, W1P OHA,
Tel: 0171 383 3555.
Information on conditions (including rare syndromes) affecting
children.

Council for Disabled Children and National Childrens' Bureau
8 Wakley Street, London, EC1V 7QE, Tel: 0171 843 6000,
Fax: 0171 278 9512.
Free information service and range of free publications, including a
list of organisations concerned with specific disabilities.

Downs Syndrome Association
155 Mitcham Road, London, SW17 9PG, Tel: 0181 682 4001.
Support and information.

Education Law Association (ELAS)
Administrator, 39 Oakleigh Avenue, London, N20 9JE,
Tel: 0181 445 6747.

Independent Panel for Special Education Advice (IPSEA)
4 Ancient House Mews, Woodbridge, Suffolk, IP12 1DH,
Tel/Fax: 01394 382 814.
Telephone advice line for parents of children with special needs,
particularly in the area of assessment and statementing. IPSEA also
has a national network of volunteers who offer second opinions,
independent assessments and, where appropriate, support and
advocacy. This is a free service.

KIDS
Kids National Office, 80 Waynflete Square, London, W10 6UD,
Tel: 0181 969 2817.
National Charity set up to provide a local service to children who
have special needs and their parents/carers.

Rathbone Society
1st Floor, The Excaliber Building, 77 Whitworth Street,
Manchester, M1 6EZ, Tel: 0161 236 5358.

Royal Institute for the Blind
Information Service, 224 Great Portland Street, London, WIN 6AA, Tel: 0171 388 1266.

Royal National Institute for the Deaf
19-23 Featherstone Street, London, EC1Y 8SL, Tel: 0171 296 8000, Text: 0171 388 6038 Minicom: 0171 383 3159.

The Dyslexia Institute
133 Gresham Road, Staines, Middlesex, TW18 2AJ, Tel: 01784 463851, Fax: 01784 460747.

The Dyspraxia Foundation
8 West Alley, Hitchin, Herts, SG5 1 EG, Tel: 01462 454986, Fax: 01462 455052.

The Law Society
113 Chancery Lane, London, WC2, Tel: 0171 242 1222. Publishes series of booklets listing solicitors who do legal aid work and other sources of legal advice.

The National Autistic Society
276 Willesden Lane, London, NW2 5RB, Tel: 0181 451 1114, Fax: 0181 451 5865.
Established to encourage a better understanding of autism, and to pioneer specialist services for people with autism and those who care for them.

The National Association for Special Educational Needs (NASEN)
4/5 Amber Business Village, Amber Close, Amington, Tamworth, Staffs, B77 4RP, Tel: 01827 311500, Fax: 01827 313005.
Promotes the development of children and young people with special educational needs and supports those who work with them.

The National Library for the Blind
Far Cromwell Road, Bredbury, Stockport, SK6 2SG, Tel: 0161 494 0217, Fax: 0161 406 6728.

MENCAP

123 Golden Lane, London, EC1Y ORT, Tel: 0171 454 0454.
Information on services for people with learning difficulties.

National Deaf Children's Society (NDCS)

15 Dufferin Street, London, EC1Y 8PD, Tel: 0171 250 0123.
An organisation of families, parents and carers which exists to
enable deaf children to maximise their skills and abilities. Through
national and regional staff they provide a range of services to
families with deaf children throughout the United Kingdom.

Network 81

1-7 Woodfield Terrace, Chapel Hill, Stansted, Essex, CM24 8AJ,
Tel: 01279 647 415.
National support organisation for parents of children with special
educational needs who want mainstream provision for their
children.

Parents in Partnership

Top Portacabin, Clare House, St George's Hospital, Blackshaw
Road, London, SW17, Tel: 0181 767 3211.
Telephone helpline. Parents help each other through local groups,
mainly in London area. Helps parents with assessment and
statementing.

People First

207-215 Kings Cross Road, London, WC1X 9DB, Tel: 0171 713
6400.
Self advocacy organisation of people with learning difficulties.

SEN Families Support Group

1a Newton Court, Newton Road, Urmston, Manchester, M41 5BA,
Tel: 0161 755 3482.
Monday to Friday 2.00 - 6.00 pm; Saturday 3.00 - 5.00 pm.

SENSE (The National Deaf Blind and Rubella Association)

11 -13 Clifton Terrace, Finsbury Park, London, N4 3SR,
Tel: 0171 272 7774

SCOPE (formerly Spastics Society)
12 Park Crescent, London, W1N 4EQ, Tel: 0171 636 5020.
Has an advisory assessment service which offers independent
multiprofessional assessment - there is a fee for this service. Some
local advocacy work.

SKILL
336 Brixton Road, London, SW9 7AA, Tel: 0171 274 0565,
Fax: 0171 264 7840.
It aims to develop opportunities for young people and adults with
disabilities and learning difficulties in further, higher and adult
education in training and the transition to employment.

The Basic Skills Agency
7th Floor, Commonwealth House, 1-19 New Oxford Street, London,
WC1A 1NU, Tel: 0171 405 4017, Fax: 0171 404 5038.
It is a national development agency for literacy, numeracy and
related basic skills.

Your local library should also have information on SEN and may be
able to put you in touch with local organisations.

Your child's school child development centre, doctor, health centre,
LEA officer, educational psychologist, learning support teacher, LEA
adviser or parent partnership officer should be able to give you useful
information and contacts.